Original title:
The Silent Winter

Copyright © 2024 Swan Charm
All rights reserved.

Author: Mirell Mesipuu
ISBN HARDBACK: 978-9908-52-086-5
ISBN PAPERBACK: 978-9908-52-087-2
ISBN EBOOK: 978-9908-52-088-9

Echoes of White Silence

Blankets of snow, soft and bright,
Whispers of calm in the night.
Frozen trees stand still with grace,
Nature's hush in this sacred space.

Footsteps muffled, quiet and light,
Moonlight dances, a ghostly sight.
Stars peek down, a silver stream,
In this realm, we softly dream.

Tranquility in the Chill

Frosted air hangs crisp and clear,
Peace envelops, drawing near.
Silent woods, a tranquil scene,
Winter's magic, pure and serene.

Branches heavy, dressed in white,
Stillness reigns, a peaceful night.
Time slows down, a gentle pause,
Nature whispers, without a cause.

Winter's Breath of Stillness

In the hush of falling snow,
Life slows down, thoughts softly flow.
Whispers linger on frozen streams,
Crystalline beauty, woven dreams.

Biting winds carry secrets old,
Stories of warmth against the cold.
In the silence, a heartbeat thrums,
Winter's breath in softening hums.

Frosty Embrace

Nature's canvas, white and wide,
A frosty embrace where dreams abide.
Lazily drifts the snowflakes' dance,
Each one unique, a fleeting chance.

Winter's chill wraps me tight,
Drawing me close in soft twilight.
In this moment, I find my peace,
A tranquil heart, where worries cease.

Soft Footsteps on Ice

A whisper glides on winter's breath,
Soft footsteps trace the frozen path.
Moonlight dances on the waning night,
Echoes of silence, a frigid light.

Beneath the chill, the world holds still,
Each step a story, each mark a thrill.
Frost-kissed blades in a silent trance,
Nature's canvas invites a glance.

In shadows long, the stars align,
Each frozen moment, a thread divine.
Here in the quiet, time seems to pause,
Soft footsteps echo, an art without flaws.

Sleepy Boughs Await

Sleepy boughs in the weight of snow,
Cradling dreams in a soft, white glow.
Beneath their cover, secrets lie,
Whispers of the winds that sigh.

They sway gently in the night's embrace,
Guarding the hush of a frozen place.
Resting softly, they hold the calm,
Nature's cradle, a tranquil balm.

When morning breaks with a golden hue,
Awake the world with a fresh debut.
Sleepy boughs, now kissed by sun,
Stirring with life, the day's begun.

Snowflakes in the Stillness

Snowflakes drift in the softest air,
Whirling gently, beyond compare.
Each a wish from the skies above,
Falling softly, a dance of love.

Carpeting earth in a silken white,
Transforming the world in gentle light.
A stillness blankets the bustling ground,
In this moment, peace is found.

Children giggle, catching the flight,
Of snowflakes swirling in pure delight.
Nature's shower, a fleeting grace,
In every flake, a soft embrace.

The Dreamer's Thaw

The dreamer's thaw in the warming sun,
Chasing shadows as the days have run.
Frosty whispers begin to fade,
Awakening life in a vibrant parade.

Buds emerge from the sleep of night,
Painting the world in colors bright.
Melodies of spring begin to play,
Gently coaxing the chill away.

The river sings of a brand new life,
As the dreamer's heart warms from strife.
Each beating pulse, a call to rise,
In the thawing dream, the spirit flies.

Time Wrapped in Snow

Gentle whispers through the trees,
Embrace the chill that brings us peace.
Moments lost in winter's grasp,
Hold them tight, let memories clasp.

Footprints vanish, soft and white,
As day falls softly into night.
Seasons shift, yet here we stand,
In dreams of frost, hand in hand.

Each flake dances, pure and light,
Carving paths in the silent night.
Time wrapped softly, a tender show,
In the arms of winter's glow.

Stillness reigns, a tranquil scene,
Veils of white, serene and clean.
Frozen moments, still and slow,
In this world, let love bestow.

Shroud of Frost

Cloaked in cold, the world lies still,
A shroud of frost, a soft, white thrill.
Nature's quilt, stitched with care,
Whispers secrets that float in air.

Trees adorned in icy lace,
Each branch a story, time won't erase.
In the hush, a breath, a sigh,
Underneath this endless sky.

Glistening shards of dawn's embrace,
A silent dance in this sacred space.
Frosty echoes, crisp and bright,
Capture moments, pure delight.

Yet as the sun begins to rise,
The shroud retreats, no more disguise.
Leaving traces, memories echoed,
In the light, the frost bestowed.

Still Waters Run Cold

Silent mirrors reflecting skies,
In tranquil depths, a stillness lies.
Amidst the chill, a whispered tale,
Of secrets held, where dreams set sail.

Beneath the surface, shadows play,
With every ripple, night and day.
Frozen edges kiss the shore,
In quiet moments, we explore.

Leaves turn to frost, a delicate art,
Nature's canvas, a beating heart.
Still waters hold the whispering breeze,
In the quiet, our souls find ease.

Echoes linger, soft and low,
In the silence, feelings grow.
Cold reflections, love unfolds,
In the quiet, still waters hold.

A Silence of Snowflakes

Every flake a soft embrace,
Dancing down, they find their place.
Whispers echo in the dark,
A silence wrapped around the park.

Gentle landings, pure and bright,
Transforming earth in silver light.
Each soft touch, a fleeting kiss,
In this calm, we find our bliss.

Shapes designed by winter's breath,
Fleeting patterns, life and death.
In this stillness, time holds fast,
A moment caught, a memory cast.

As dawn breaks, shadows play,
In the light, the snowflakes sway.
Stillness speaks, with silent grace,
In the silence, we find our place.

Winter's Gentle Murmur

Snowflakes dance on whispered breeze,
Holding secrets of the freeze.
Branches sway, a soft embrace,
Nature's calm, a tranquil space.

Footprints left in powdery white,
Stories fade with falling light.
Crisp air holds a fleeting sound,
Winter's grace all around.

Silent nights, the world asleep,
Dreams in drifts, so soft and deep.
Stars above, a shimmering touch,
Guiding hearts that long for much.

Fires crackle, warmth inside,
Memories bloom, like the tide.
Hot cocoa and laughter shared,
Love that lingers, deeply cared.

In the stillness of the night,
Hope emerges, pure and bright.
Winter's murmur softly calls,
Embracing joy as snowfall falls.

Boundless White

A canvas vast, all draped in snow,
Where time stands still, and breezes blow.
Mountains rise, majestic, grand,
Nature's beauty, a silent hand.

Footprints trace a fleeting tale,
Of wanderers that brave the pale.
Winter's breath, a frosty kiss,
In every flake, a touch of bliss.

Chill wraps round like a soft sigh,
The world adorned, a lullaby.
Skyward dreams, a boundless flight,
In this realm of endless white.

Whispers echo through the trees,
Carried on the frozen breeze.
Glimmers of light, a soft parade,
In winter's hush, all fears do fade.

Together wrapped in warmth we find,
The essence of a love entwined.
In this white, a canvas true,
Endless moments shared with you.

Traces of a Quiet Year

Beneath the snow, the silence deep,
Memories linger, secrets keep.
Time unfolds in gentle waves,
As winter's chill, the heart still braves.

Each flake falls like a whispered prayer,
Tracing paths of love laid bare.
Through the hush, a longing breath,
In quiet echoes, life and death.

Frosty windows, stories told,
Of fleeting moments, young and old.
Candles flicker, shadows dance,
In the stillness, hearts find chance.

A year concludes, a soft goodbye,
As twilight paints the evening sky.
Hope renews, with winter's end,
In time's embrace, we start to mend.

With each dawn, a blank new page,
Traces etched, wisdom of age.
Quiet years that softly pass,
We gather love, like fallen glass.

Frost-Kissed Memories

Mirror lakes in morning glow,
Reflecting dreams from long ago.
Frosted trees in silent cheer,
Whispers of the past draw near.

Colors muted, soft and pale,
Each moment dances, like a tale.
Echoes of laughter fill the air,
Frost-kissed memories everywhere.

Blankets warm against the chill,
Time slows down, a gentle thrill.
In every breath, a story spun,
Of days well spent, and love begun.

Through the window, winter's blush,
In every flake, a velvet hush.
Captured time, forever strong,
In frost-kissed moments, we belong.

When seasons change and days grow bright,
We'll hold these memories, pure delight.
In winter's heart, our stories weave,
Frost-kissed dreams, we still believe.

Hibernation of Whispered Thoughts

In shadows deep, the silence grows,
As winter wraps the world in snow.
Whispers linger, soft and shy,
Awaiting spring to lift the sigh.

The dreams lie still, like frozen streams,
Beneath the blanket of night's dreams.
Each thought a snowflake, resting light,
In hibernation's tender night.

Beneath the stars, the mind will stay,
In quiet calm, in soft ballet.
The whispers thrumming, deep and low,
Await the warmth, the gentle glow.

As nature sleeps, so too the heart,
In slumber deep, a place to start.
When morning comes, the sunlight beams,
Awakening all the silent dreams.

The time will end, the frost will fade,
With every kiss of warmth displayed.
The whispered thoughts will rise anew,
In vibrant life, in colors true.

Ghostly Silence of the Night

In shadows cast by silver light,
The world is hushed, a gentle sight.
A ghostly calm enfolds the air,
As time suspends its heavy care.

The moon peeks through the trees so tall,
With whispers soft, it makes its call.
In secret glades where echoes play,
The night unveils her dreams in gray.

Each rustle speaks of tales long lost,
A haunting breath that bears the cost.
In silence deep, the heart will know,
The world's embrace, both sweet and slow.

The stars collide in cosmic dance,
While shadows weave a dark romance.
In the stillness, thoughts take flight,
Through the ghostly silence of the night.

As dawn approaches, colors choke,
The fleeting dreams, a tender cloak.
Yet in the calm, a truth remains,
The ghostly silence still retains.

Muffled Hearts Beneath Layers

In whispers soft, the snowflakes fall,
Hiding secrets, muffled call.
Beneath the cold, our warmth remains,
In silent beats, love's gentle chains.

Through frosted panes, we seek the light,
Each breath we share, a soft delight.
Wrapped in layers, hearts entwined,
In quiet moments, souls aligned.

Winter's cloak, a heavy sheet,
Yet in its fold, our spirits meet.
Beneath the frost, the fire glows,
In muffled hearts, warmth still flows.

We tread on paths, where silence dwells,
And in each step, our story swells.
Gathered close, our laughter rings,
As time stands still, with all it brings.

So here we stay, as seasons shift,
In quietude, we find the gift.
Muffled hearts beneath the snow,
In love's embrace, we'll always grow.

Shadows of the Pine and Snow

Midday light breaks through the trees,
Casting shadows with gentle ease.
Where pine boughs whisper, secrets hide,
In this sanctuary, we confide.

Snow blankets ground in silence deep,
While hidden dreams in slumber keep.
Nature's hush, a breathing space,
Among the pines, we find our place.

Cold winds dance through branches tall,
Echoing stories, a haunting call.
Yet here we stand, two hearts as one,
Beneath the sky, where dreams are spun.

The crisp air bites, yet we feel whole,
United warmth, the heart and soul.
Each moment shared, an endless flow,
In shadows cast by pine and snow.

As twilight falls, the world transforms,
In gentle grace, as beauty warms.
Together, we embrace the night,
In shadows deep, our hearts take flight.

A Canvas of Unspoken Frost

A canvas white, the world adorned,
With secrets shared, yet never worn.
Each flake a whisper, soft and bright,
Painting dreams in the pale moonlight.

Frost-kissed branches, silver lace,
Nature's brush in a quiet space.
Unsaid words hang like icicles,
In silent beauty, time reveals.

We wander through this frozen maze,
Each step a dance, a fleeting gaze.
In unison, the world we trace,
Two spirits bound, in winter's grace.

The whispering winds, a lullaby,
As the sun dips low, the stars draw nigh.
In this moment, everything's clear,
A canvas vast, where love draws near.

So let the frost embrace our hearts,
In every breath, a work of art.
With each heartbeat, let love stay,
On this canvas, come what may.

The Stillness Between Winters

Between the storms, a quiet pause,
Where time stands still, without a cause.
In muted tones, the world does sigh,
As all is calm beneath the sky.

The lingering chill of winter's breath,
Hints at whispers from beyond death.
Yet in this hush, a promise waits,
For spring's arrival, and opened gates.

Trees stand bare, but life remains,
In tender buds, hidden refrains.
Awaiting warmth, the earth holds tight,
In stillness, dreaming of the light.

The silence speaks in gentle threads,
Connecting all that lives and spreads.
In every heartbeat, nature's song,
A sacred bond, where we belong.

So let us cherish quiet's grace,
In the stillness, find our place.
Between the winters, we will thrive,
As hope and love keep dreams alive.

Moonlit Silence

In the night so calm and deep,
The moonlight weaves a dream to keep.
Stars twinkle like whispers above,
Wrapped in silence, the world we love.

Shadows dance on the forest floor,
Each rustle holds secrets in store.
Soft breezes carry a gentle sigh,
As the night paints the canvas high.

Owls call from the ancient trees,
A haunting melody floats on the breeze.
Nature's heart beats slow and true,
In this quiet space, only for you.

The silver glow embraces all,
In its warmth, I feel so small.
Time pauses in this serene night,
Cradled gently in soft moonlight.

With each breath, the magic grows,
In moonlit silence, anything goes.
As dreams unfold and spirits blend,
It's here in stillness, we find our mend.

Frosted Breath

Morning breaks with a chilly bite,
Breath of frost sparkles in the light.
Nature shivers, dressed in white,
Awakening under winter's might.

Trees wear coats of glistening ice,
Each twig a diamond, oh so nice.
Footsteps crunch on the frozen ground,
In this crisp stillness, peace is found.

The brook whispers beneath its shell,
A quiet secret it yearns to tell.
Frosted whispers dance on the air,
Cascading moments beyond compare.

Sunrise paints the canvas bright,
Melting frost in the warming light.
Winter bows to the day's embrace,
Yet holds a memory in its grace.

As the day fades, the chill returns,
A frosted breath, as evening learns.
Wrapped in blankets, we find our rest,
In the heart of winter's quiet fest.

Stillness Underneath

Beneath the surface, calm does lie,
Where shadows wait and whispers sigh.
Time flows gently, a hidden stream,
In stillness, we chase the dream.

Layers deep, the stories wait,
Bound by silence, they celebrate.
Roots entwine, a timeless thread,
In quiet moments, life is fed.

The earth's heartbeat, soft and low,
Guides us gently, we follow slow.
In the dark, a promise sleeps,
Awakening when the silence weeps.

Troubles fade like dust on air,
In stillness, there's magic rare.
Nature's pulse, steady and true,
Reminds us of what we once knew.

Hold your breath, listen near,
In the hush, find what is dear.
Stillness speaks in quiet tones,
In its embrace, we're never alone.

Frosted Echoes

Echoes linger in the quiet air,
Frosted whispers dance without care.
Footprints trace a tale untold,
In the snowy blanket, life unfolds.

The morning light paints the scene,
Frosted crystals, a silver sheen.
Each breath lingers, crisp and clear,
Echoes of nature, drawing near.

Branches bow with weighty grace,
Carrying the chill in their embrace.
As time slows in winter's grasp,
Frosted echoes, like a gentle clasp.

Underneath the silent sky,
Dreams take flight, as seasons sigh.
In the stillness, find your way,
Let frosted echoes softly sway.

As dusk calls, the shadows play,
Night returns to steal the day.
In their frost, the night winds weave,
Echoes of winter, quietly breathe.

Beneath the Frosted Sky

Silent whispers fill the air,
Stars like jewels, shining rare.
Moonlight casts a silver glow,
Beneath the frost, the world moves slow.

Trees adorned in icy lace,
Nature wears a still embrace.
Footprints crunching on the ground,
In this peace, calm is found.

Snowflakes dance on gentle breeze,
Bringing magic, aiming to please.
Every breath, a frosty plume,
Nestled in winter's quiet room.

Time drifts by in soft repose,
Wrapped in warmth, as the cold blows.
Beneath the frost, life quietly stirs,
In the hush, the heart infers.

As daylight fades, the colors blend,
Creating beauty that will not end.
In this moment, frozen and bright,
Beneath the frosted sky tonight.

Enchanted Winter's Rest

Glistening fields, untouched white,
Blanket of snow, pure and bright.
The world pauses, takes a breath,
In this stillness, echoes of death.

Quietude wraps the earth in peace,
Nature holds its sweet release.
With every flake, a story told,
As winter's embrace turns hearts to gold.

Underneath the serene expanse,
Dreams awaken, begin to dance.
Branches heavy, stoop and bend,
In this quiet, souls can mend.

Fires crackle, warmth inside,
As the world outside will bide.
Hot cocoa in hand, time unwinds,
In enchanted winter, joy reminds.

Stars twinkle with a gentle grace,
As night falls, we find our place.
In the hush, love's light will last,
In winter's rest, we hold it fast.

Cold Snap Reveries

Chill winds blow, whispers low,
Dreams like snowflakes gently flow.
Underneath the frozen sky,
Echoes of laughter linger nigh.

Frosted branches, a sight divine,
Nature adorned in winter's line.
Each breath visible, hangs in air,
A moment captured, beyond compare.

Memories swirl like flakes that fall,
In the quiet, we hear the call.
Softly swirling, thoughts meander,
In this magic, we can wander.

Night descends, stars shine bright,
In the cold, we seek the light.
Holding close what matters most,
Finding warmth in the winter's ghost.

Dreams take flight in the frosty breeze,
As the world rests with such ease.
In cold snap reveries we find,
The warmth of peace within our mind.

A Time for Stillness

Beneath the veil of winter's gloom,
A quiet heart begins to bloom.
Each moment wrapped in silver white,
A time for stillness, soft and light.

Snowflakes whisper their gentle song,
Painting landscapes, pure and strong.
The world slows down, takes a pause,
Nature's rhythm, without cause.

In the hush, the soul can breathe,
Letting go of what we grieve.
Footsteps echo on the trail,
In this calm, our spirits sail.

The flicker of a candle glows,
In quiet corners, warmth bestows.
As night wraps 'round, we find our peace,
In stillness, worries start to cease.

A time for stillness, hearts unite,
In winter's arms, everything feels right.
With each heartbeat, we find our way,
In the calm of the winter day.

Frostbitten Whispers

Whispers drift through the trees,
Softly freezing your breath,
Nature's secrets on the breeze,
Caught in winter's gentle death.

Footsteps crunch on the ground,
Echoes linger in the cold,
Silent stories all around,
In the stillness, feelings bold.

Silver shadows dance with glee,
Underneath the pale moonlight,
Frostbitten dreams, wild and free,
In the heart of the winter night.

Softly glimmers in the dark,
Stars like frost on velvet sky,
Each one holds a winter spark,
Whispers of the who and why.

In the chill, I find my peace,
Fractured thoughts begin to mend,
Nature's art, a sweet release,
Frostbitten whispers never end.

Stillness Wrapped in White

Stillness wrapped in blankets white,
Snowflakes dance and twirl with grace,
Nature's canvas pure and bright,
A frosty hush fills every space.

Branches glisten, silvered glow,
Quietude reigns over the land,
In the stillness, feelings grow,
As winter's touch lends a hand.

The world slows down, time stands still,
Memories wrapped in sheets of frost,
In this moment, a gentle thrill,
In the stillness, love is lost.

Footprints trace a winding path,
Leading toward the unknown way,
In the calm, feel winter's wrath,
Yet here, all worries drift away.

Stillness whispers in the night,
Wrapped in warmth of dreams so bright,
In the snow's embrace, take flight,
This winter's tale, a soft delight.

Secrets Hidden in the Drift

Secrets buried deep in snow,
Hold the stories yet untold,
Beneath the blankets, soft and slow,
Whispers of the brave and bold.

Frozen echoes of the past,
Layered deep in winter's grace,
Moments lost but meant to last,
In the quiet, time does trace.

Winds conceal the truth we seek,
With every gust, a tale unfolds,
Silent voices, soft and meek,
In the drift, the heart beholds.

Stillness reigns in twilight's glimmer,
Crystals sparkle on the ground,
In the dusk, our hopes grow slimmer,
Yet in secrets, warmth is found.

As night descends, the world will sigh,
And dreams are wrapped in winter's gift,
With every breath, a whispered cry,
For secrets hidden in the drift.

Echoes of a Frosty Dawn

Echoes call with morning light,
Frosted air is crisp and clear,
A new day breaks, bidding night,
In the silence, dreams appear.

Sunlight kisses snowflakes bright,
Painting hills in silver gold,
Nature wakes with soft delight,
As its beauty is retold.

Gentle whispers through the pines,
Chill and warmth in harmony,
Echoes soft as moonlight shines,
Holding all that's meant to be.

Frosty dawn, a canvas wide,
Where the day and night collide,
Each moment holds a chance to glide,
Into dreams where hopes abide.

As the echoes fade away,
Morning breathes a thawing tune,
In its arms, we dare to play,
Underneath the watchful moon.

Shimmering Frost

Frosty breath on morning air,
Whispers dance with gentle care.
Sparkling jewels on every tree,
Nature's gift, serene and free.

Sunrise paints the world below,
Crystalline in golden glow.
Each blade shines, a diamond's face,
In this winter's sweet embrace.

Footsteps crunch on icy ground,
Silence reigns, no other sound.
Every breath a misty plume,
In this still and frosty room.

Branches draped in silver lace,
Time slows down, a slower pace.
Winter's magic, pure and bright,
Shimmers softly in the light.

At dusk the sky begins to change,
Colors shift, a soft exchange.
Twilight whispers, night appears,
Frosty tales dissolve our fears.

A Canvas of White Quiet

A blanket pure, the world transformed,
In silence deep, all life is warmed.
Each flake unique, a fragile gift,
A canvas wide where shadows drift.

Cotton clouds afloat in blue,
All around, each path anew.
Footprints left in powder white,
Echoes soft by fading light.

Trees wear coats of winter's grace,
Stillness holds this sacred space.
A hush that wraps the earth so tight,
Every heartbeat feels just right.

In icy streams, reflections play,
Colors dance in cold array.
Moonlight weaves through branches bare,
Casting dreams in frosty air.

Night descends, the stars ignite,
Glistening gems on velvet night.
Shadows stretch, the world is still,
Wrapped in white, a tranquil thrill.

Still Air and Cold Stars

Underneath a blanket dark,
Whispers drift, an ancient spark.
Stars like diamonds in the night,
Quiet stories taking flight.

Pine trees stand with hearts of stone,
In this realm, we are alone.
Chill embraces skin and bone,
In the stillness, thoughts have grown.

Frozen breath in crisp, clean air,
Every moment demands a stare.
A hush falls over all we see,
Boundless, vast infinity.

Silver craters on the moon,
Silent lullabies a tune.
Night unfurls her velvet shawl,
In her grasp, we feel so small.

Still air hums a lullaby,
As frost paints dreams across the sky.
In moments still, our spirits roam,
Finding peace, we feel at home.

A Veil of Ice

Life slowed down beneath the dome,
A veil of ice, a frozen home.
Each surface smooth, a glassy sheen,
Nature's art, so pure, serene.

Windows glinting in the light,
Frames adorned like winter's night.
In this world, all seems to stop,
Frozen moments, time will drop.

Softly falls a gentle snow,
Wrapping earth in quiet glow.
Hushed are whispers, stilled the strife,
In this realm, we breathe pure life.

Icicles hanging from the eaves,
Nature's chandeliers, like leaves.
Crisp and clear, the world is bright,
Within this glimmer, brings delight.

Brisk winds tease and twist the night,
As shadows slip from sight.
A veil of ice, a frosty trance,
In its wonder, we take a chance.

The Art of Winter's Quiet

Silence whispers through the trees,
As snowflakes dance upon the breeze.
Nature's pause, serene and slow,
Where dreams emerge in glistened glow.

Beneath the blanket, earth is still,
A tranquil peace, a muted thrill.
Footsteps echo soft and light,
In the heart of winter's night.

Frosted windows, breath of cold,
Stories of the past unfold.
The world transforms in white embrace,
In winter's art, we find our place.

Branches heavy, laden dreams,
Captured soft in silver beams.
Time stands still, as moments weave,
In the quiet, we believe.

Night descends, a gentle shroud,
Underneath, all fears are cowed.
In every flake, a wish is spun,
The art of winter has begun.

Tranquility in the Snowfall

In falling snow, the world finds peace,
A soothing balm, a sweet release.
Each flake a note in nature's score,
An orchestra that we adore.

The streets are hushed, the lights aglow,
As winter paints with softest flow.
A canvas bright, yet dimly lit,
In this stillness, we quietly sit.

Footprints left in crystal white,
Trace our path that feels so right.
The chill wraps close, a warm retreat,
In tranquility, our hearts meet.

Wind whispers secrets through the air,
A gentle touch of icy care.
With every breath, the beauty grows,
In the snowfall, tranquility flows.

Stars peek through the fluffy veil,
Guiding dreams where hopes prevail.
In the hush of night's embrace,
We find our calm in winter's grace.

Shadows of Quietude

In the stillness, shadows creep,
As winter settles in to sleep.
Bare branches reach toward the night,
Whispering secrets, soft and light.

Moonlight dances on the snow,
Casting magic, soft and slow.
Every corner, every space,
Holds a story, a sacred place.

Windsong carries through the air,
A quiet note, a tranquil prayer.
In the shadows, silence sings,
Of dormant dreams and timeless things.

Frosty edges, crisp and clear,
Bring the warmth of those we hold dear.
In the dark, we find our way,
Guided by the dreams of day.

Here in quietude, we reflect,
On life and love, we reconnect.
Each shadow holds a gentle sigh,
A lullaby beneath the sky.

Requiem of the Frost-laden Trees

Amidst the boughs, the frost does cling,
A carol sung by winter's wing.
Each branch adorned like a crown,
Whispers memories, softly drown.

Silvery limbs, a graceful bow,
Holding secrets, etched in snow.
In their stillness, tales unfold,
Of winters past, of hearts consoled.

With every gust, a sigh is drawn,
In the twilight, heralds dawn.
Frost-laden dreams in twilight glow,
Embrace the warmth from hearts we know.

Resilient trees stand tall and brave,
In winter's grip, their souls they save.
Each frozen leaf a silent prayer,
For life and love, beyond despair.

In the chill, their stories weave,
A requiem, where we believe.
Through frost and cold, they come alive,
In nature's stillness, they survive.

Shadows of Slumber

In the hush of twilight's fade,
Whispers weave through dreams' parade.
Dancing softly, shadows play,
Cradled in the arms of gray.

Stars emerge like distant sighs,
Beneath the blanket of dark skies.
Lullabies of night begin,
As slumber's veil wraps all within.

Moonbeams cast their gentle light,
Guiding hearts through the quiet night.
Every secret softly spoken,
In the stillness, no dreams broken.

Time stands still in this embrace,
Where worries fade without a trace.
Live the magic, feel the peace,
In shadows where our minds release.

As dawn creeps in, dreams must flee,
Yet in the night, we feel so free.
Embrace the dark, let barriers fall,
For in shadows, we find our all.

Ghosts of Evergreen

In the forest, whispers call,
Echoes of the past to all.
Gentle rustling of the leaves,
Where the spirit often weaves.

Misty trails and shadows blend,
Every corner holds a friend.
Old trees dance with graceful sway,
Ghosts of those who lost their way.

Silence hangs like fragile lace,
In this timeless, sacred space.
Crickets sing their twilight tune,
Underneath the watchful moon.

Every footstep, a story told,
In the warmth of soft green mold.
Each breath brings the past to life,
In the woodlands, joy and strife.

Lost in dreams of yesteryear,
The echoes whisper ever near.
In the embrace of ancient trees,
We find comfort in memories.

Breath of the Frozen Night

In the stillness, chilled and bright,
Lies the breath of frozen night.
Stars like crystals in the air,
Frozen wonders everywhere.

Wind sings low through frosted pines,
Whispers secrets, ancient signs.
Moonlight bathes the world in white,
Painting shadows, pure delight.

Footsteps marked in softest snow,
Where the glistening flurries flow.
Every breath, a cloud in sight,
Carried forth by cold's invite.

Nature's hush, a calming blend,
Night's embrace, a gentle friend.
In this quiet, hearts take flight,
Captured by the frozen night.

Time dissolves in winter's haze,
Lost within the silver craze.
In the grasp of cold's caress,
We find warmth in the wilderness.

Quietude in the Cold

In the stillness, silence reigns,
Embracing all, soothing pains.
Frozen landscapes, crisp with grace,
Nature's touch, a calm embrace.

Beneath the snow, life waits anew,
Hiding dreams in frosty dew.
Whispers of the wind, a song,
In the stillness, we belong.

Stars shine bright in deep blue skies,
Glistening like our deepest sighs.
In the chill, we find a spark,
Quietude, a sacred arc.

Fires crackle, warmth inside,
While outside, snowflakes dance and glide.
Every moment, pure and bold,
In the peace of winter's hold.

Soon the thaw will greet the dawn,
Yet in cold, our hearts have drawn.
In the quiet, we find our way,
Embraced by winter, night, and day.

Veils of Winter's Breath

A whispering chill in the air,
Soft flakes begin to fall,
Nature dons a silken white,
As silence blankets all.

Trees wear coats of frosted lace,
Branches bow with grace,
Footsteps crunch on frozen ground,
Winter's magic in this place.

The river sings in murmurs low,
Its breath a gentle freeze,
Reflecting skies of iron gray,
Wrapped in winter's tease.

Hushed are the sounds of summer's thrill,
As night drapes its shawl,
In the quiet, frosty breath,
Nature answers winter's call.

With fireside glow and hot cocoa,
Hearts warm amidst the frost,
Embracing love in chilly nights,
In winter's arms, we're lost.

The Frosted Horizon

Over hills, a shimmer lies,
Blankets soft and white,
The dawn breaks in pastel hues,
Chasing away the night.

Clouds adorned with glimmered dust,
Kisses from the sun,
Every shadow bends and sways,
As day and winter run.

Far-off peaks in silver light,
Stand proud against the blue,
Their secrets held in frozen freeze,
Draped in a frosted hue.

The winds whisper tales of old,
Of winters yet to come,
The horizon smiles softly now,
Within the frosty drum.

As dusk begins to weave its veil,
Stars peek through the gray,
The world a canvas, pure and bright,
At the frosted break of day.

In the Quiet Light

The world slows down in gentle sighs,
As twilight softly glows,
In the quiet light of dusk,
A tranquil beauty flows.

Snowflakes dance on winter's breath,
Painting scenes so pure,
Every corner, small and large,
Wrapped in a moment's allure.

Soft shadows stretch across the land,
While colors slowly fade,
With whispers of the coming stars,
In this silent serenade.

The snow drapes paths like gentle dreams,
Where footsteps lightly tread,
In the peaceful harmony,
Of the stories left unsaid.

In the quiet light, we find our peace,
With hearts that bask and sway,
In every moment, still and bright,
As night consumes the day.

Twilight in Tundra

The sun dips low in golden hue,
The sky a canvas wide,
In tundra's realm, the cold winds blow,
As day begins to hide.

Crisp air fills the twilight chill,
A serenade of frost,
Echoes of the distant stars,
In beauty, we are lost.

Echoes of the Arctic howl,
Through icy, barren trees,
Every breath of winter's song,
A dance upon the breeze.

Colors shimmer, dimmed and bright,
As shadows stretch with grace,
In this twilight, nature's heart,
Finds peace in its embrace.

As the stars emerge like dreams,
On velvet canvas, lie,
Twilight wraps the tundra tight,
Beneath the cosmic sky.

Still Waters in Winterscape

Beneath the frost, the river sleeps,
Its surface glints, a secret keeps.
Branches bow, adorned in white,
A tranquil world, so pure, so bright.

Footsteps hush on snowy banks,
Silent whispers, nature's pranks.
Reflections dance in icy hue,
In stillness, life renews anew.

The sky drapes low, a muted gray,
While snowflakes waltz in gentle sway.
Each breath a mist, the air so clear,
In winter's grasp, we hold it dear.

Among the reeds, a world confined,
In frozen moments, peace we find.
Echoes of warmth in hearts remain,
Still waters hum a soft refrain.

Harmony of the Frozen Air

In chilling breeze, the silence sings,
Notes of winter, the joy it brings.
Trees like shadows, tall and proud,
Whisper soft beneath a shroud.

Every breath its own refrain,
The harmony of crisp, clear pain.
Ice-kissed blooms, their beauty rare,
In this wonder, we cease care.

Stars above like diamonds glow,
Glistening on the fields of snow.
Nature's music, soft and grand,
In the frozen air, we stand.

Each flake a note, a fleeting sound,
Together weave a joy profound.
In the stillness, the heart will soar,
Harmony calls forevermore.

A Pause in the Winter Song

Listen close, the world holds breath,
A winter hush that speaks of death.
Nature still, in snowy shroud,
Each moment sings, though not aloud.

Time stands still on frozen ground,
In the quiet, peace is found.
Branches bow to whisper low,
A pause in the dance of snow.

The brook beneath the ice does flow,
Hidden secrets, soft and slow.
Winter's voice, a gentle sigh,
In the stillness, dreams amplify.

With every flake, a story spun,
Of long-lost warmth and brighter sun.
A moment grasped, before it's gone,
This pause in the winter song.

Slumbering Earth Beneath a White Cloak

Beneath the snow, the earth does dream,
Wrapped in white, a silent theme.
Roots embrace the winter's chill,
In deep repose, the world stands still.

Mountains rise, adorned in grace,
While time retreats at winter's pace.
The landscape glows, a ghostly white,
A slumbering earth, a soft delight.

Hills like pillows, soft and round,
In this crystal realm, peace is found.
Only the stars above will know,
The whispers held in layers of snow.

Dreams of spring lie deep within,
Where life awaits for warmth to begin.
But for now, in stillness, we bask,
In winter's cloak, a gentle task.

Hushed Echoes of December

Whispers dance on frosty air,
Softly ringing everywhere.
Silent steps on powdered snow,
Winter's secrets, hushed and low.

Twilight drapes a silver shroud,
Wrapping nature in a cloud.
Trees adorned in crystal lace,
Hold the warmth of a hidden place.

Fires crackle in homes so bright,
Casting shadows, soft and light.
Memories flood like gentle streams,
Wrapped in warm and tender dreams.

Nights are long, yet hearts are near,
In this time, we hold what's dear.
Laughs and stories by the flame,
In the chill, we speak your name.

As December whispers clear,
Promises of love appear.
In the stillness, feel the glow,
Hushed echoes only we will know.

Muted Crystals Under Moonlight

Moonlight spills on silent fields,
Nature's magic gently yields.
Crystals glimmer, softly bright,
Whispers carried by the night.

Each flake falls with graceful ease,
Draping earth in quiet peace.
Colors fade, but spirits rise,
Underneath the starlit skies.

Shadows play among the trees,
Carried on the night's soft breeze.
Footsteps hidden, quiet, small,
In the stillness, hear the call.

Silent lullabies take flight,
Wrapped in warmth, a pure delight.
Every crystal holds a dream,
Mirrored in the silver stream.

In this realm of soft embrace,
Find your heart's most cherished place.
Though the winter night may chill,
In its beauty, find your will.

Beneath the Surface of Ice

Quiet depths hold secrets old,
Beneath the ice, stories told.
Frozen whispers, time stands still,
Waiting for the sun to fill.

Life stirs gently, hidden deep,
In the silence, dreams still sleep.
Bubbles rise like thoughts of past,
Underneath, shadows are cast.

Patterns form, a lace-like sheen,
Nature's canvas, pure and keen.
Echoes of what used to be,
Frozen moments, wild and free.

Each crack sings of life anew,
Waiting for the warmth to come through.
Spring will break the cold away,
Revealing truth of yesterday.

So we wait, beneath the ice,
For the thaw, the sweet reprise.
In the stillness, patience grows,
Beneath the ice, the river flows.

Elegy for the Snowbound

Fields of white stretch far and wide,
In the silence, dreams abide.
Frozen visions paint the sky,
While the winds of winter sigh.

Each flake falls, a whispered prayer,
Tender moments light the air.
Echoing of souls once known,
In the midst, we feel alone.

Time stands still in snowy gloom,
Each breath veils a fleeting room.
Memories wrapped in soft, cold dust,
In the silence, find your trust.

Shadows linger, lost in thought,
Feelings cherished, battles fought.
Through the snowbound, time goes by,
In the stillness, hear the cry.

Yet within this winter's woe,
Lies a bond that still will grow.
In the quiet, love will bloom,
Even 'neath the eternal gloom.

Lanterns in a Blizzard

Snowflakes dance in chilly air,
Lanterns glow with tender care.
Whispers lost in winter's breath,
Hope ignites amid the death.

Shadows flicker, softly made,
In the night, a solace laid.
Footsteps crunch on frosty ground,
In the dark, warm hearts abound.

Winds howl like ghosts of old,
Stories in the darkness told.
Through the storm, a light remains,
Guiding souls through icy pains.

Each lantern sways in ghostly light,
Casting dreams into the night.
Through the blizzard, dreams still soar,
Illuminating hope once more.

As nature sleeps beneath the snow,
The lanterns' warmth will always glow.
In the blizzard, we unite,
In the cold, we'll find our light.

When Time is Frozen

In the stillness of the night,
Where moments halt and fade from sight.
Chronicles whisper, yet remain,
In silence, feelings alter strain.

Frosty clocks suspended high,
Starlit dreams that never die.
When seconds blend into the haze,
Time's embrace a gentle maze.

Echoes echo all around,
In this place, lost time is found.
Minds entwined in endless thought,
Frozen moments, battles fought.

Shadows linger, past forgot,
In the stillness, there is not.
Life drifts softly, like a sigh,
In the freeze, we learn to fly.

When the heart learns how to wait,
In the stillness, we create.
Frozen time, a sacred ground,
In the pause, our joy is found.

Nature's Drowsy Heart

Beneath a veil of morning mist,
Nature stirs, but not insist.
Dreaming deep in slumbered grace,
Softly wrapped in time and space.

Whispers of the waking dawn,
Gentle songs of life reborn.
Branches sway in sleepy yawn,
As the world waits for the morn.

Flowers peek from frozen earth,
In their bloom, a quiet mirth.
Nature's heart, a lullaby,
In her arms, the echoes fly.

Clouds drift low, a drifting dream,
Softly stirring, waters gleam.
In the hush of waking light,
Nature's breath, a wondrous sight.

As the sun breaks through the gray,
Night's soft shadows melt away.
In her drowsy, pulsing rhythm,
Nature hums a tranquil hymn.

Tranquil Icicles

Hanging glistens, winter's art,
Icicles dance, serene and smart.
Dripping crystal, nature's tears,
Reflecting strength throughout the years.

From rooftops, they dangle bright,
Silent sentries in the night.
In the calm of frosty air,
Spirits whisper, softly rare.

Each drop falls with a gentle grace,
Time pauses in this frozen space.
A world adorned in crystal hues,
Nature sings her silent blues.

Icicles, like hopes, they gleam,
In the sun, they softly beam.
Holding dreams in fragile charm,
In their quiet, there's no harm.

As they melt beneath the sun,
Change arrives, but not a run.
In transitions, find the peace,
Tranquil moments never cease.

Chilled Whispers

In the frost's soft embrace,
Whispers dance through the air,
Secrets woven in silence,
Gentle touch everywhere.

Moonlight bathes the still night,
Casting shadows like dreams,
Every breath a cold story,
Lost in silvery beams.

Trees stand tall, wise and old,
Guardians of winter's lore,
Their branches, like fingers, hold
The whispers of yore.

Steps crunch softly on snow,
Each echo a fleeting chance,
To hear the night's lullaby,
In this frozen expanse.

As dawn spreads its warm glow,
The whispers begin to fade,
Yet their chill lingers on,
In the hearts where they stayed.

A Fable in White

Once upon a soft night,
A blanket of snow fell deep,
Every creature within sight,
Cuddled close in their sleep.

The trees told tales of old,
In whispers soft as a sigh,
Of brave hearts, fierce and bold,
Underneath the vast sky.

A rabbit danced through the fields,
With dreams of the sunlit days,
While the night, in silence, yields,
To its wondrous, snowy maze.

The stars blinked in delight,
And the moon kept watch above,
Painting stories in white,
With the magic of love.

A fable woven in dreams,
In the hush of the calm night,
Nature sings soft, it seems,
Of hope, pure and bright.

Solitude Wrapped in Snow

In the quiet of the night,
Snowflakes drift and sway,
A blanket soft and white,
Hiding all the fray.

Footsteps fade in the dark,
Echoes lost in the chill,
The world, a silent park,
Time stands still and still.

Solitude weaves its charm,
Embracing the earth tight,
With a soft, soothing balm,
Wrapped in winter's white.

Moonbeams dance on the snow,
Casting shadows so rare,
In this moment, let go,
Of worries, of despair.

Here in the snowy peace,
Find solace in the night,
Let your heart find release,
In solitude's sweet light.

The Echo of Hibernation

Beneath the layers of snow,
Creatures sleep sound and deep,
Through winter's lull they flow,
In dreams, they quietly creep.

The world slows down its pace,
Nature holds its breath tight,
Cradled in winter's grace,
Wrapped in soft, shimmering white.

Whispers of ice and frost,
Tell tales of days gone by,
In this season of loss,
New beginnings still lie.

The echo, soft and low,
Of life beneath the snow,
Reminds us to rest well,
In the stillness, we grow.

For each moment in pause,
A promise of spring's song,
In the echo's gentle laws,
We learn where we belong.

Whispers of Frost

In the quiet of dawn's first light,
Whispers of frost take gentle flight.
Each blade of grass wears a crystal crown,
Nature's breath soft, without a sound.

Mist curls slow in the morning glow,
Hiding secrets that the cold winds know.
A fleeting touch on the winter's breath,
Whispers of life, though faced with death.

Trees stand tall, their branches white,
Guardians of silence, holding tight.
The world transformed, serene and still,
Each frosted whisper a test of will.

As the sun climbs high and warms the earth,
The frost retreats, revealing birth.
Yet in its wake, the silence stays,
Whispers of frost in morning's rays.

With every step on the frozen ground,
A soft crunch echoes, a sacred sound.
In the hush of winter, we find our peace,
Whispers of frost that never cease.

Veil of Crystal Dreams

Underneath a veil of night,
Crystal dreams take sudden flight.
Each star a whisper in the dark,
Guiding hearts to leave their mark.

Moonlight weaves through branches bare,
Casting shadows in the air.
A dance of hopes from far away,
Carried softly till break of day.

In the silence, secrets gleam,
Life and death, a fragile theme.
Within this dream, all fears fade,
In such beauty, hearts are laid.

Frozen moments of blissful grace,
The world adorned in a soft embrace.
Each breath of night a silent song,
Veil of dreams where we belong.

When dawn breaks, the magic fades,
Yet in memory, the beauty stays.
A trace of night's ethereal seam,
In our hearts, the crystal dream.

Echoes in the Snow

Footsteps fall on blankets white,
Echoes linger in morning light.
Each crunch a tale, a moment's past,
In winter's grasp, quiet and vast.

The trees stand guard, their branches low,
Holding secrets deep in snow.
Each flake a whisper, soft and clear,
Echoes of joy, of love, of fear.

As the cold winds dance and weave,
Nature holds what we believe.
In stillness found, we see it grow,
Life's soft echoes in the snow.

Stars peek out from skies of gray,
Guiding dreams that drift away.
In this moment, time feels slow,
Each heartbeat sings in the snow.

When night descends, the world is hushed,
Echoes of life in silence brushed.
Yet in the quiet, souls will flow,
Finding warmth in the winter's glow.

Hushed Landscapes

Across the hills, a blanket lies,
Hushed landscapes under winter skies.
The world asleep, in soft embrace,
Nature holds its quiet grace.

Crisp air filled with a serene sigh,
As clouds float low, and spirits fly.
Whispers dance on gentle winds,
In every corner, magic begins.

Mountains bow in tranquil peace,
Where time pauses, and worries cease.
Each glance reveals a sacred art,
Hushed landscapes, a dreamer's heart.

Snowflakes twirl like whispered words,
Spreading joy among the birds.
Hope alights in every flake,
In this stillness, dreams awake.

Embracing silence, life unfolds,
Through the stillness, stories told.
In nature's arms, we find our place,
Hushed landscapes, a warm embrace.

A Veil of Clouds and Silence

Softly draped in morning mist,
Whispers echo, softly kissed.
Shapes in shadow, pale and shy,
Clouds above drift, dreams on high.

Silence holds the world in sway,
As the dawning breaks the gray.
Each breath lingers, time stands still,
In this realm of calm and will.

Nature's secrets softly weave,
In the air, the heart believes.
Thoughts like feathers float and soar,
In this quiet, we explore.

Horizon blushes, subtle hue,
Slowly melting, fresh and new.
Veil of clouds, a gentle shroud,
Cradles dreams, both soft and loud.

As the day unfolds its wings,
With the hope that sunlight brings.
In this quiet, truth resides,
Where the heart forever glides.

Solitude in the White Embrace

Snowflakes dance on winter's breath,
A cloak of white, a silent death.
Footprints print the untouched ground,
In this stillness, peace is found.

Trees are hushed in frosted grace,
Nature wears a soft, white lace.
Each breath clouds in cold air's kiss,
Moments wrapped in tranquil bliss.

Whispers wander through the night,
Stars above, a distant light.
In the vastness of the frost,
Love is gained, and never lost.

Solitude, a loyal friend,
In the silence, hearts can mend.
Every flake a story told,
In the quiet, bold and cold.

Beneath the moon's soft, watchful eye,
Loneliness begins to fly.
In this embrace, we discover,
Winter's beauty, like a lover.

Crystal Silence in the Night

Nightscape painted with a brush,
Stars ignite in fleeting hush.
Moonlight spills on silver seas,
Whispers buzzing with the breeze.

Beneath the glow, shadows crawl,
Embrace of silence, deep and tall.
Crystal clarity fills the air,
In this void, we softly stare.

Each twinkling light a distant tale,
Nights like this, we cannot fail.
Glimmers flicker, dreams unfold,
In the dark, the heart feels bold.

Echoes linger from afar,
Silent songs, a guiding star.
In the stillness, thoughts ignite,
Creating worlds in crystal night.

All around, the time slows down,
In this peace, we will not drown.
With every star that lights the sky,
Whisper to the night, and fly.

Solitary Footprints in Snow

A trail blazed through soft, white ground,
Each footprint speaks without a sound.
In the still, the heart can roam,
Wandering far from the known home.

Crisp air bites, yet warmth persists,
In solitude's gentle trysts.
Snowflakes fall and gently kiss,
Every moment wrapped in bliss.

Barren branches, stark and bare,
Tell stories in the wintry air.
Silence reigns, a sacred law,
Embraced in nature's gentle claw.

Footprints lead to places new,
Where wonders wait for me and you.
Each step takes us deeper still,
Into dreams of quiet will.

Solitary, yet not alone,
In this silence, seeds are sown.
With each step, the journey grows,
In the snow, the heart bestows.

The Dance of Snowflakes

Snowflakes twirl in winter's air,
Their gentle spins without a care.
Each one unique, a soft ballet,
They shimmer bright, then drift away.

In swirling gusts, they laugh and glide,
Painting the earth, a pure white tide.
They dance upon the frozen ground,
In silent waltz, no other sound.

The world around, a canvas bright,
Transformed by winter's pure delight.
They gather close, a feathery quilt,
A tranquil scene, in beauty built.

As dusk falls down, they gleam and shine,
Reflecting stars, a gift divine.
In every flake, a story told,
Of winter's grace, a sight to hold.

Bow down the trees, their boughs adorned,
With icy gems, the day reborn.
In moonlit glow, they softly gleam,
Snowflakes dance like a fleeting dream.

Beyond the Snowdrifts

Beyond the mounds of crisp white snow,
Lies a hidden world, few come to know.
Footprints whisper, secrets untold,
In the stillness, adventures unfold.

Crisp branches sway in evening's grasp,
They hold the tales of winter's clasp.
Beneath the drifts, life holds its breath,
In nature's dance, there's beauty in death.

The sun peeks through, a golden ray,
It melts the chill, paves the way.
For buds to bloom and life to stir,
Beyond the snowdrifts, spring will occur.

A world awakened from winter's dream,
With colors bright, a joyful scream.
Yet still it holds, a quiet grace,
The beauty born from snow's embrace.

Beyond these mounds, we find our way,
To seek the warmth of brighter day.
In each fleeting moment, life will thrive,
Beyond the snowdrifts, we feel alive.

Whispers of Frost

Whispers of frost on morning leaves,
Tell tales of nights that winter weaves.
A breath of chill in the muted dawn,
As nature stirs, the stillness drawn.

The icy patterns, delicate lace,
Adorn the world, a quiet grace.
They sparkle bright in the soft sunlight,
Each crystal formed, just right, just right.

In hidden corners, secrets lay,
Frost-kissed beauty, here to stay.
As shadows stretch and daylight grows,
The whispers fade, but magic flows.

The song of frost, a gentle tune,
Echoes softly beneath the moon.
In every breath, a promise lies,
In winter's heart, the spring will rise.

So listen close, to nature's rhyme,
The whispers of frost will hold their time.
In moments still, a truth we find,
In winter's chill, our hearts unwind.

Veils of Stillness

Veils of stillness cloak the night,
Wrapped in shadows, soft and light.
The world at rest, a silent sigh,
As stars twinkle in the endless sky.

A blanket thick with quiet grace,
Hides the chaos, time and space.
In whispered winds, the secrets flow,
Through nights adorned with glimmers low.

Each breath we take, like snowflakes fall,
In hushed tones, we hear winter's call.
The moon's soft glow, a guardian bright,
Guides our dreams through the tranquil night.

With each new dawn, the stillness breaks,
The world awakens, and new life wakes.
Yet in our hearts, the echo stays,
Of veils of stillness, in twilight's haze.

So let us pause, embrace the calm,
Within the quiet, there's a balm.
In stillness found, we come to know,
The beauty lies where time moves slow.

Silence Beneath the Pines

In the shade where whispers dwell,
The pines stand tall, a sentinel.
Soft winds carry secrets low,
Nature's peace, a gentle flow.

Sunlight dapples through the green,
A tranquil world, so serene.
Beneath the boughs, all is still,
In this calm, the heart can fill.

Rustling leaves in harmony,
Singing sweetly, wild and free.
Nature's voice, a soothing sound,
In this haven, lost, I'm found.

Beasts of earth roam without fear,
In this silence, they draw near.
Every rustle, every sigh,
A testament to peace nearby.

Beneath the pines, I close my eyes,
Dreaming under painted skies.
A world of quiet, deep and wide,
Where nature's truths and dreams abide.

Crystalline Reflections

In the stillness of the night,
Moonbeams dance in purest light.
Crystals shimmer, silver bright,
Nature's jewels, a wondrous sight.

Water's surface, smooth and clear,
Mirroring all that is near.
Gentle ripples hint away,
Secrets hidden in the sway.

Stars above like diamonds glow,
Guiding where the waters flow.
Each reflection tells a tale,
In this shimmering, tranquil vale.

Breath of night, so crisp and cold,
The world transforms, a sight to behold.
Dreams are woven, hearts take flight,
In crystalline reflections, pure delight.

Time stands still, lost in the scene,
The beauty of the calm serene.
With every glance, the heart connects,
To nature's art, love's effects.

The Frosted Horizon

When dawn breaks with a frosty kiss,
A world transformed, a moment of bliss.
Each blade of grass, a crystal crown,
A winter's spell, wrapping the town.

Sky painted in hues of pale blue,
While chilly winds whisper anew.
Mountains stand in their icy grace,
Guardians of this frozen space.

Footsteps crunch on the pure white ground,
A symphony of winter's sound.
Snowflakes twirl in playful dance,
Enchanting all in winter's trance.

Sunrise casts a golden glow,
Transforming frost to sparkling snow.
Every corner, every rise,
A magical world that mesmerizes.

In this realm where silence sings,
Nature's beauty stirs our wings.
The frosted horizon, vast and bright,
Awakens joy with morning light.

Veiled in Snow

A blanket soft, white as dreams,
Covers earth in gentle seams.
Trees adorned in winter's lace,
Nature's pause, a tranquil space.

Whispers linger in the air,
Promises of beauty rare.
Each flake tells a tale of grace,
In the stillness, life's embrace.

Footprints lost in deep, white drifts,
Time stands still, the spirit lifts.
Breezes sing of joys untold,
In this wonderland of cold.

Sunshine glimmers on the peaks,
Nature's brush, its art still speaks.
Veiled in snow, the world retreats,
Finding peace where stillness meets.

Beauty wrapped in frost and light,
In the quiet, hearts take flight.
Veiled in snow, the soul finds home,
In winter's arms, no need to roam.

The Lullaby of Thaw

The ice begins to melt away,
As flowers stretch towards the day.
Whispers of spring in the breeze,
Nature awakens, seeks to please.

Streams that once were frozen tight,
Glisten softly in the light.
Birds return with joyful song,
Their melodies where they belong.

Underneath the warming sun,
Life resumes, the season's fun.
Gentle rains will start to fall,
Nature sings its sweet install.

A canvas painted fresh and bright,
Colors bursting, pure delight.
Each moment brings a new surprise,
Hope and joy before our eyes.

As day turns into evening's glow,
The world transforms beneath the flow.
A lullaby of soft refrains,
The thaw begins, our heart regains.

Starlit Shivers

Underneath a velvet sky,
Stars like diamonds, oh so high.
Whispers cool the night air still,
Magic time, a moment's thrill.

Shadows dance, the moonlight glows,
Secrets that the night bestows.
Breezes carry tales of old,
Stories of love brightly told.

A shooting star streaks the night,
Wishes made in pure delight.
Serenade of softest dreams,
Awakened by the silver beams.

Embrace the chill that lingers near,
Every shiver holds a fear.
Yet in the dark, we find our grace,
In starlit skies, we'll find our place.

With every beat, the heart will soar,
Dancing on the twilight's floor.
Starlit shivers, a soul's embrace,
In the night, we find our space.

Beneath a Blanket of White

Gentle flakes fall from the sky,
Whispers soft, as they drift by.
Covering the world so deep,
In the silence, dreams will seep.

Fields now wrapped in luminous hue,
Nature's peace, a tranquil view.
Footsteps crunch on winter's cloak,
In this silence, hearts evoke.

Children's laughter echoes clear,
Building snowmen, full of cheer.
Snowballs fly, in gleeful plays,
Joyful shouts in snowy bays.

Beneath the moon's soft, silver light,
Frosted trees, a charming sight.
Each moment wrapped in quiet bliss,
In this winter's gentle kiss.

Warmth of firesides, tales to share,
Hot cocoa cups, the cozy air.
Underneath this blanket's hold,
Winter's magic, pure and bold.

Serene Snowfall

The world transforms as white descends,
A hush that only nature lends.
Flakes like feathers drift and sway,
In a dance, they find their way.

Every corner dressed in dreams,
Silent nights where starlight gleams.
Softly falling, time stands still,
A canvas brushed with winter's will.

Branches mask their winter wear,
Crystals glowing, everywhere.
Every flake a story told,
In the stillness, dreams unfold.

Serene snowfall, hearts embrace,
In the chill, we find our grace.
Moments shared, each breath is bright,
Wrapped in peace, a pure delight.

As dawn awakens, soft and slow,
The world is kissed in glimmers low.
Each snowfall brings a chance to heed,
A serenade to every need.

Dreamscapes of the Icy Still

In the hush of frost-kissed nights,
Visions dance in silver light,
Silent whispers softly call,
As frozen dreams begin to thrall.

Crystals shimmer, stars align,
Nature's canvas, pure, divine,
In the stillness, hearts take flight,
Through the veil of endless white.

Mysteries in shadows lie,
Beneath the moon's enchanted sigh,
Echoes linger, barely heard,
In this realm where night is blurred.

Time suspended, breaths held still,
In this land of icy chill,
All that's known begins to fade,
In the dreams that winter made.

From the depths of dreams we rise,
Beneath the vast and starry skies,
In the quiet, we belong,
In the stillness, we are strong.

Quietude in a Tundra of Silence

Amidst the vast and snowy plains,
A solitude that gently reigns,
Echoes stir where no one goes,
In the hush, each moment flows.

Bare branches stretch against the gloom,
In the silence, frost will bloom,
Thoughts drift softly, like the snow,
In the stillness, hearts will grow.

Footsteps muffled, whispers low,
In this land where shadows grow,
Time is woven, thread by thread,
In the quiet, we are led.

Snowflakes falling, soft and light,
Wrapping all in purest white,
Cradled close, we sense the space,
In the frozen, we find grace.

As the world holds its breath tight,
In this tundra, hearts ignite,
Finding warmth in silent song,
In the stillness, we belong.

Whispers of a Chilling Embrace

Beneath the blaze of winter's moon,
Softly sung, a gentle tune,
Cold winds weave through empty trees,
Carrying whispers, laced with freeze.

Hands outstretched to catch the air,
In this magic, light and rare,
Frosty fingers touch the skin,
Like a secret held within.

Stars above, a twinkling crown,
In the silence, we won't drown,
Every breath a crystal sight,
In the dark, we feel the light.

Embraced within the chilling night,
Hearts entwined, a bond so tight,
In each stillness, love will find,
A warmth that echoes in the mind.

As the world succumbs to sleep,
In this stillness, promises keep,
Whispers linger, shadows play,
In the cold, we bloom and sway.

Echoes of the Falling Snow

In a world draped soft in white,
Snowflakes dance in gentle flight,
Each one whispers, tales of old,
In their beauty, stories told.

Frosted breaths collide with air,
Chasing dreams without a care,
Every flake that meets the ground,
Speaks of secrets that abound.

Nature cradles time in snow,
Memories in silence grow,
Amidst the still, a pulse we feel,
In this moment, hearts reveal.

Through the night, the echoes sing,
In their song, our hopes take wing,
With each drift, our spirits rise,
In the snow, we find the skies.

As dawn breaks, a new day calls,
Snowflakes glisten, softly falls,
In the winter's gentle glow,
We find hope in falling snow.

Embrace of the Cold Twilight

As daylight fades, shadows creep,
In twilight's arms, the secrets keep.
Stars awaken, a silent song,
In the night's embrace, we belong.

Cold whispers dance through the trees,
Carrying tales on the icy breeze.
The moon hangs low, a silver thread,
Guiding dreams as we drift to bed.

A frost-kissed touch on weary cheeks,
In the stillness, the heart speaks.
Crystals glisten on branches bare,
Nature's canvas, beyond compare.

Time slows down in this serene light,
Wrapped in the hush of the approaching night.
Embracing shadows, nothing to fear,
In the cold twilight, all becomes clear.

With every breath, a vapored sigh,
Underneath the vast, endless sky.
In this moment, we find our hold,
In the embrace of the cold twilight, bold.

Lullabies of the Icy Wind

Hear the lullabies softly sung,
By the icy wind, forever young.
Whispers of snowflakes gently fall,
Nature's serenade, enchanting all.

In the stillness, the world retreats,
Wrapped in layers, warmth completes.
As branches sway, a soothing tune,
Under the watchful gaze of the moon.

Frozen murmurs through forests deep,
In this realm, all secrets keep.
The breath of winter, soft yet clear,
Brings calmness that all hearts revere.

With every gust, a story flows,
Of distant lands and long-lost woes.
Through the night, a gentle guide,
In the embrace of winter, we confide.

As dreams take flight on this chilly breeze,
The icy wind brings us to our knees.
In harmony, our souls entwine,
To the lullabies of the icy wind, divine.

Silent Sentinels of the North

Beneath the sky, the sentinels stand,
Guardians of the frozen land.
With stoic grace, they softly rise,
Under the gaze of endless skies.

Veiled in snow, their presence grand,
Whispering secrets across the sand.
Their branches stretch, a timeless reach,
In silence, life teaches what they preach.

The frost adorned, a shimmering crown,
Upon each head, winter's gown.
In solitude, they silently keep,
Watchful eyes, while the world sleeps.

With every storm, they bend and sway,
Yet strong they stand, come what may.
Silent sentinels, wise and old,
Telling stories only the night has told.

In the stillness, we hear their call,
Echoing softly, embracing all.
In the realm of ice, they truly dwell,
Silent sentinels, guardians of all that's well.

Forgotten Dreams of the Cold

In the depths of winter's hold,
Lie forgotten dreams, a tale untold.
Frosty echoes of what once was,
In the heart, their yearning does pause.

Crystalline wishes, lost in time,
Whispers of hope, a silent rhyme.
As the snow blankets the earth so deep,
Feed the memories, secrets to keep.

Each flake that falls, a story spun,
Of battles fought, of races run.
In the quiet, where shadows blend,
Forgotten dreams learn to mend.

With the chill comes a higher thought,
In solitude, wisdom is sought.
In the cold, our spirits strive,
To bring forth what keeps us alive.

So let the frost kiss your skin,
Reviving dreams long buried within.
In the silence, we find gold,
In forgotten dreams of the cold.

Nature's Naptime

Whispers of the trees so deep,
Softly cradle the earth to sleep.
Gentle breezes, a soft sigh,
Nature's lullaby drifts by.

Flowers bow as daylight fades,
In the forest, calm cascades.
Crickets chirp a sweet refrain,
As shadows weave in dappled grain.

The brook hums low, a soothing stream,
Carrying dreams down its gleam.
Moonlit paths where silence creeps,
Embracing all in tender keeps.

Stars awaken in the night,
Casting glimmers, soft and bright.
Nature rests, her heart aglow,
In the hush of twilight's flow.

Secluded Serenity

Hidden nooks, where silence dwells,
Nature's secrets, quiet spells.
Soft moss cushions the weary feet,
In this refuge, time's discreet.

Birdsong flutters through the pines,
Crafting peace in greening vines.
Here the worries fade away,
As the heart begins to sway.

Dappled sunlight gently plays,
On the ground where the stillness stays.
Rippling waters sing in tune,
Wrapped in dreams beneath the moon.

Each breath a gift, a tender pause,
In nature's arms, without a cause.
Secluded space, a healing balm,
In tranquil whispers, pure and calm.

Moonbeams on Ice

Glittering crystals, pure and bright,
Moonbeams dance on frosty night.
Whispers of winter brush the ground,
In magic silence, beauty found.

A tranquil world, veiled in white,
Where shadows play in silver light.
Each flake drifts down, a soft caress,
Glistening wonders, nature's dress.

Footprints trace a story told,
As icy wonders slowly unfold.
Stars above in a velvet sky,
Glowing softly, as dreams drift by.

Time slows down in this chill embrace,
Wrapped in warmth, a sacred space.
Moonbeams shining on the ice,
Whispering softly, they entice.

Slumber of the Earth

In twilight's hush, the world subsides,
Embracing night, where silence hides.
The earth whispers a gentle sigh,
As stars awaken in the sky.

Fields wrapped in blankets of soft dew,
Rest beneath the sky so blue.
Mountains stand as sentinels tall,
Guarding dreams that softly fall.

The moon casts a silver glow,
On sleeping rivers, calm and slow.
Nature's heart beats soft and low,
In the slumber, peace will grow.

Beneath the surface, life awaits,
In quiet chambers, fate creates.
Awaiting spring's warm, tender breath,
In the stillness, life finds its depth.

Veiled by Snowflakes' Dance

Gentle flurries swirl around,
A silent waltz on winter ground.
Softly they kiss the earth so white,
As day drifts softly into night.

Each flake a story yet untold,
In the cool embrace, we feel so bold.
They wrap the world in purest grace,
In this cold, enchanted space.

Trees stand tall, adorned in white,
Branches glisten, a warming sight.
Nature's beauty captured slow,
In the magic of the snow.

Beneath them lies an unseen ground,
Where secrets of the past abound.
Whispers of warmth, dreams take flight,
In this timed pause of winter's light.

As night descends and stars appear,
The snowflakes dance, we hold them dear.
In their gentle touch, we find peace,
And let our worries find release.

When Time Holds Its Breath

Caught in the stillness, hearts align,
Moments linger, become divine.
As shadows stretch and silence grows,
The world awaits, the stillness flows.

In twilight's grasp, all seems to cease,
A fleeting thought, a sense of peace.
Time's whisper soft, so soft to hear,
Echoes linger, drawing near.

With breaths held tight, we pause, reflect,
On paths well walked, on time perfect.
Eyes closed gently, we embrace light,
In this embrace, the dark takes flight.

Colors fade into the night,
Stars emerge, a wondrous sight.
When stillness reigns, the soul takes wing,
In revered silence, lost in spring.

A moment trapped in endless sense,
When time stands still, it feels immense.
The dance of life in quiet grace,
Awaits us all in this sacred space.

Icicle Reflections of Emptiness

Hanging from eaves, silent gleams,
Icicles catch the sun's lost beams.
Frigid forms of hollow shells,
Echoes of unspoken spells.

Crystal daggers poised to fall,
Nature's art, a chilling call.
In their stillness, stories freeze,
Of empty nights and whispered pleas.

Beneath them lies a fragile truth,
Fractured dreams of fleeting youth.
The world in ice, a paradox,
As warmth retreats and silence locks.

In their depths, the void reflects,
A longing heart that life rejects.
Yet beauty rests amongst the cold,
In every shard, a tale unfolds.

So gaze upon the icicle's face,
And find the void, the empty space.
In stillness, clarity is found,
In every silence, whispered sound.

Whispering Pines in a Frozen Hush

Amid the woods, the pines stand tall,
Whispers weave through their spired thrall.
A frozen hush, where secrets reign,
In nature's breath, a soft refrain.

Snow-laden branches bow with grace,
Holding stillness in this space.
Through needles green, the silence flows,
In winter's heart, the quiet grows.

The world beyond is lost, unseen,
Here, every footfall feels serene.
An echo stirs with every breeze,
Whispered tales in frozen trees.

Underneath a blanket white,
Life stirs slowly, out of sight.
In the stillness, hope will bloom,
When winter's grip begins to loom.

So pause a while, in pines, be still,
Feel the magic, the quiet thrill.
In whispers soft, let nature speak,
In frozen hush, find warmth we seek.

Secrets of the Snowy Landscape

Whispers of frost in the dawn's first light,
Blankets of white, a breathtaking sight.
Footprints of creatures dance in the glow,
Nature's secrets lie deep below.

Trees stand guard with their icy attire,
Veils of snow, like a delicate choir.
Mountains echo tales from days of yore,
In the silence, we long to explore.

Crystal shards glint in the sun's embrace,
The hidden paths in this tranquil space.
Clouds drift gently, a soft ballet,
In the snowy expanse where dreams play.

The brook sings quietly, cloaked in white,
Under the stars, a serene night.
Each flake a story, each drift a clue,
In the snowy landscape, old and new.

Secrets unveiled in the winter chill,
Nature's wonders, a world to fulfill.
In the stillness, our hearts align,
Lost in the beauty, so divine.

Quieting the World

Stillness envelops where chaos once reigned,
Moments of peace in the silence attained.
Whispers of nature, a calming refrain,
Quieting the world, easing the pain.

Leaves flutter gently in the softest breeze,
Time slows down, granting sweet release.
Clouds above drift with effortless grace,
In this refuge, we find our place.

Birdsongs fade into the muted air,
In the hush, all burdens we can spare.
Stars gently twinkle, a celestial guide,
In quietude, we no longer hide.

The heartbeat of earth, a timeless beat,
In tranquil moments, our souls can meet.
Steps of serenity on the forest floor,
Quieting the world, forevermore.

As dusk descends, the colors blend,
In silence, our spirit finds its mend.
Wrapped in the lull of the evening's gray,
Quieting the world, come what may.

Dreams on Frozen Ground

Under a blanket of shimmering ice,
Whispers of dreams, both tender and nice.
Footprints of hope in the frostbitten air,
Dancing on dreams, free from despair.

The moon casts shadows on the silvery plains,
While the snowflakes waltz like delicate chains.
Stars above paint the night sky with glee,
Inviting our hearts to dream wild and free.

Every breath congeals in the frosty night,
Laughter and echo emerge in the light.
In the stillness, we dare to believe,
That dreams on frozen ground can achieve.

Fields of white cradle the fantasies gleamed,
In shimmering silence, a world that had dreamed.
Hope frozen yet warm, as soft as a sigh,
Together we rest where our dreams can fly.

Awake in the stillness, the night whispers soft,
Carried on breezes, our spirits aloft.
In the heart of the frost, let imagination surge,
Dreams on frozen ground begin to emerge.

The Sound of Silence

In the hush of the night, whispers abide,
A canvas of quiet where shadows confide.
Invisible echoes paint stories profound,
In the depths of the calm, the lost can be found.

Each breath is a treasure, a moment in time,
Yearning for stillness, a rhythm, a rhyme.
Softness envelops, inviting the mind,
To wander in spaces where peace we can find.

Stars twinkle gently, a symphony bright,
Conducted by silence, shunning the light.
The world takes a pause, its heartbeat slows down,
In the sound of silence, we wear a new crown.

Thoughts drift on air, like feathers in flight,
During moments of grace that linger at night.
In the serenade of shadows we bask,
In the sound of silence, our souls can unmask.

Let go of worries, surrender your wrath,
In quiet reflections, embrace the still path.
For in that deep silence, love's whispers arise,
The sound of silence, a gift in disguise.

Memories Breathed into the Chill

Whispers of the past, they sigh,
Carried softly, a winter's cry.
Footprints linger in the snow,
Echoes of moments long ago.

Frozen laughter, shadows cast,
Embers of joys that fade so fast.
A breath held tight, a fleeting glance,
In this chill, we dance our trance.

Silent trees in moonlit grace,
Guarding stories time won't erase.
Each flake a memory, pure and bright,
In the quiet, we search for light.

Time drifts like smoke, lost in air,
In the stillness, we find repair.
Embracing warmth in frosty night,
Memories breathe, hearts take flight.

In the chill, our spirits blend,
Threads of the past, they never end.
Frosty breath, a gentle kiss,
Moments captured in this bliss.

The Beauty of a Soundless Night

Stars ignite the heavens wide,
In the hush, the worlds abide.
Soft whispers of night's embrace,
Dreams unravel in this space.

Moonbeams dance on silent streams,
Painting shadows, kindling dreams.
A symphony of quiet sighs,
Beneath the vast and watchful skies.

Every breath a fleeting prayer,
Gravity pulls us unaware.
The beauty in a muted tone,
In the stillness, we're not alone.

A blanket of stars, vast and deep,
In this calm, our secrets keep.
Time drifts slow, moments ignite,
The beauty of a soundless night.

In the dark, our hearts alight,
Finding solace, pure delight.
Wrapped in warmth of silence found,
In these shadows, we're unbound.

Secrets Crystallized in White

Snowflakes whisper tales of old,
Tiny secrets, stories told.
Each one unique, a gentle sight,
Crystallized in purest white.

Frozen breath upon the air,
Cloaks of mystery everywhere.
Though the world feels hushed and shy,
In these secrets, wonders lie.

Glimmers caught in icy streams,
Where the heart can weave its dreams.
Layered softly, truth and light,
Wrapped in whispers, pure and bright.

As the night unfolds its veil,
In the silence, we unveil.
Memories like frost take flight,
Secrets crystallized in white.

Yearning hearts beneath the snow,
Holding treasures soft and slow.
In this calm, lost dreams ignite,
For in stillness, all feels right.

Frosted Reflections of Solitude

Windows freeze with thoughts unseen,
Framed in dreams that softly glean.
A world held still, in silver light,
Frosted reflections of the night.

Lonely paths lined with snow,
Silent whispers, feelings flow.
In the quiet, thoughts align,
Bridges built in frost divine.

Moments linger, time's embrace,
In this solitude, we trace.
Heartbeats echo, soft and slow,
In the stillness, we learn to grow.

Every breath a gift of peace,
In these shadows, doubts release.
Eternity in frosted sight,
Reflections shimmering in light.

In solitude, there's grace anew,
A world apart, just me and you.
Frosted reflections gently weave,
In this stillness, we believe.

Chill of the Unspoken

In whispered winds, the secrets lie,
Veils of silence softly sigh.
Words unvoiced, yet heavy still,
Embrace the night with a frosty chill.

Moonlit shadows dance away,
Beneath the stars where dreams delay.
A heart that knows, yet chooses mute,
Yearns to break, but finds no root.

Every glance a silent plea,
In the dark, what could it be?
The echo lingers in the air,
Chilling truths we seldom share.

Frosted branches, bare and stark,
Nature holds its breath in dark.
Yet beneath this icy dome,
Lie emotions far from home.

So linger here, in twilight's breath,
Where warmth may hide, defying death.
Chill of unspoken, weaves and spins,
A tapestry of shadows, thick with sins.

Murmurs Beneath the Snow

Softly falling, flakes align,
Whispers dance on winter's spine.
Underneath, the earth holds tight,
Dreams cocooned in frostbit light.

Silence wraps the world in white,
While stars twinkle, pure and bright.
Hidden tales in drifts do sleep,
Secrets kept, and shadows creep.

The murmurs of the buried past,
In icy clutch, they hold steadfast.
Echoes from the roots below,
Beneath the weight, they gently flow.

Crystals glisten, veiling earth,
In this quiet, lies rebirth.
Life awaits the thawing sun,
In silent whispers, we're all one.

Murmurs rise like morning mist,
From layers deep, we can't resist.
A serenade of soft refrain,
Beneath the snow, hopes rise again.

Shush of the Frozen Realm

Frozen moments in crystal sheen,
Nature hushed, serene and keen.
The world stands still, in silent awe,
Awakening dreams we often saw.

Frigid breath on winter's face,
Time holds still in this vast space.
Shivers travel through the trees,
As if to whisper with the breeze.

In this realm where echoes hide,
Shush of secrets held inside.
Beneath the ice, a pulse remains,
Waiting for release from chains.

Frosty whispers weave the air,
Hidden stories everywhere.
In frozen stillness, shadows play,
As night gives way to dawning day.

Shush of the realm, let silence sing,
Of the beauty that calm can bring.
In every flake and silent sound,
Life's quiet song is ever found.

Shadows in the Quiet Thaw

As winter wanes, the whispers start,
Shadows linger, soft and art.
In the melting of the cold,
Stories of the past unfold.

Tender light through branches peeks,
Awakening the world that speaks.
In the puddles, reflections play,
Signs of life return in sway.

Beneath the surface, pulse revives,
As ice retreats, the heart survives.
Fingers reach for warmth outside,
In the thaw, new hopes abide.

Fragrant blooms begin to rise,
Underneath the painted skies.
Shadows dance in daylight's touch,
A world reborn, we crave so much.

Quiet thaw, with gentle grace,
Reclaims the life in every space.
In these shadows, joy appears,
A celebration through the years.

www.ingramcontent.com/pod-product-compliance
Ingram Content Group UK Ltd.
Pitfield, Milton Keynes, MK11 3LW, UK
UKHW031955131224
452403UK00010B/554